MICHAEL SOUTHERN

Echoes of War: Healing the Wounds of PTSD

Contents

I

Dedication

This book is dedicated to my brother-in-arms,

Nathaniel D. Helmuth
Sgt. US Army
July 24th, 1981 – January 6th, 2018
Severe Traumatic Brain Injury
Your courage, sacrifice, and unwavering commitment to duty will never be forgotten. Your resilience in the face of adversity continues to inspire me every day. May your legacy live on as a beacon of hope and strength to all who face the challenges of war and its aftermath. You will always hold a special place in my heart. There is not a day that goes by that I don't think about you. Miss you, Brother. Thank you for always having my back. I'm dedicating this in your name.

1

Understanding PTSD: A Veteran's Perspective

Defining PTSD: A Closer Look

PTSD, or post-traumatic stress disorder, is a mental health condition that can develop after experiencing a traumatic event. For military veterans, the risk of developing PTSD is especially high due to the nature of their service. PTSD can manifest in various ways, including flashbacks, nightmares, severe anxiety, and intrusive thoughts about the traumatic event. It is important for veterans to understand that PTSD is a normal response to abnormal circumstances and seeking help is crucial in managing the symptoms.

Many veterans may struggle with the stigma surrounding mental health issues, including PTSD. They may feel ashamed or weak for experiencing symptoms of PTSD, leading them to avoid seeking help. However, it is important for veterans to remember that seeking treatment is a sign of strength, not weakness. PTSD is a legitimate medical condition that requires professional intervention in order to effectively manage symptoms and improve overall well-being.

In order to effectively address PTSD in military veterans, it is crucial to first understand the unique challenges they face. Military service often involves exposure to extreme stress, violence, and loss, all of which can contribute to the development of PTSD. Additionally, veterans may face challenges reintegrating into civilian life, which can exacerbate symptoms of PTSD. By acknowledging these challenges and providing targeted support, veterans can better navigate the complexities of living with PTSD.

It is important for military veterans to know that they are not alone in their struggle with PTSD. There are numerous resources available to help veterans cope with their symptoms and improve their quality of life. From therapy and support groups to medication and alternative treatments, there are many options for veterans to explore in their journey toward healing. By reaching out for help and connecting with others who have shared experiences, veterans can find hope and support in their recovery from PTSD.

In conclusion, PTSD is a serious and complex condition that affects many military veterans. By understanding the nature of PTSD and seeking appropriate treatment, veterans can effectively manage their symptoms and improve their overall well-being. It is important for veterans to remember that seeking help is a sign of strength, not weakness and that there are resources available to support them in their journey towards healing. Together, we can work towards breaking the stigma surrounding PTSD and ensuring that all veterans receive the care and support they deserve.

The Impact of Trauma on Mental Health

For military veterans, the impact of trauma on mental health is a very real and serious issue. Many veterans experience post-traumatic stress disorder (PTSD) as a result of their time in combat or other traumatic situations. This can manifest in a variety of ways, including flashbacks, nightmares, and severe anxiety. These symptoms can have a profound impact on a veteran's mental health and overall well-being.

One of the key ways that trauma affects mental health is by causing changes in the brain. When a person experiences trauma, it can alter the way the brain processes information and regulates emotions. This can lead to difficulties with memory, concentration, and emotional regulation. For veterans with PTSD, these changes can make it difficult to function in everyday life and can contribute to feelings of isolation and hopelessness.

In addition to the physical changes in the brain, trauma can also have a profound impact on a veteran's emotional and psychological well-being. Many veterans with PTSD struggle with feelings of guilt, shame, and anger related to their traumatic experiences. These emotions can be overwhelming and can make it difficult for veterans to seek help or connect with others. This can further exacerbate feelings of loneliness and isolation, leading to a cycle of negative thoughts and emotions.

The impact of trauma on mental health can also have long-term consequences for veterans. Untreated PTSD can increase the risk of other mental health issues, such as depression, anxiety, and substance abuse. It can also affect a veteran's ability to hold down a job, maintain relationships, and enjoy a high quality of life. By understanding the impact of trauma on mental health, veterans can take steps to seek help and support to address their PTSD and improve their overall well-being.

In "Echoes of War: Healing the Wounds of PTSD," we explore the impact of trauma on mental health in-depth, providing insights and strategies for military veterans struggling with PTSD. Through personal stories and expert advice, we aim to help veterans understand and cope with the effects of trauma on their mental health. By recognizing the signs and symptoms of PTSD and seeking help when needed, veterans can take control of their mental health and begin the journey toward healing and recovery.

Recognizing PTSD Symptoms and Signs

As military veterans, it is important for us to be aware of the symptoms and signs of Post-Traumatic Stress Disorder (PTSD). This chapter will provide you with the knowledge and tools to recognize when you or a fellow veteran may be experiencing PTSD.

Finally, it is important to recognize the emotional symptoms of PTSD. This can include feelings of guilt, shame, anger, or sadness that are difficult to shake. If you find yourself experiencing intense emotions that interfere with your daily life, it may be a sign that you are dealing with PTSD.

One of the most common symptoms of PTSD is experiencing flashbacks or nightmares related to traumatic events. These can be triggered by certain sights, sounds, or smells that remind you of the trauma. If you find yourself reliving these events in your mind, it may be a sign that you are struggling with PTSD.

Another symptom to look out for is avoidance behavior. This can manifest as avoiding certain places, people, or activities that remind you of the traumatic event. If you find yourself withdrawing from social situations or activities that you used to enjoy, it may be a sign that you are dealing with PTSD.

Many veterans also experience heightened anxiety and hyper-vigilance as a result of their PTSD. This can manifest as feeling on edge or easily startled, as well as having difficulty sleeping or concentrating. If you find yourself constantly on guard or feeling anxious for no apparent reason, it may be a sign that you are struggling with PTSD

In conclusion, recognizing the symptoms and signs of PTSD is the first step towards getting the help and support you need. By being aware of these warning signs, you can take control of your mental health and begin the journey towards healing. Remember, you are not alone in this battle, and there is help available for you.

2

The Manifestations of PTSD

Physical Symptoms of PTSD

PTSD, or post-traumatic stress disorder, is a mental health condition that affects many military veterans. While the emotional and psychological symptoms of PTSD are often discussed, it is important to also recognize the physical symptoms that can accompany this disorder. Understanding these physical symptoms can help veterans better manage their condition and seek appropriate treatment.

One common physical symptom of PTSD is chronic pain. Veterans with PTSD may experience unexplained aches and pains throughout their body, which can be debilitating and difficult to manage. This chronic pain can be a result of the body's response to stress and trauma, and can significantly impact a veteran's quality of life. It is important for veterans to seek medical attention for their chronic pain and work with healthcare professionals to develop a treatment plan.

Another physical symptom of PTSD is insomnia. Many veterans with PTSD struggle to get a good night's sleep, which can lead to a host of physical health issues. Insomnia can worsen chronic pain, impair cognitive function, and weaken the immune system. It is crucial for veterans to prioritize their sleep and seek support from medical professionals to address their insomnia.

In addition to chronic pain and insomnia, veterans with PTSD may also experience gastrointestinal issues. Stress and trauma can disrupt the functioning of the digestive system, leading to symptoms such as stomach pain, bloating, and diarrhea. These gastrointestinal issues can be distressing and impact a veteran's overall well-being. Seeking treatment from a healthcare provider and practicing stress-reducing techniques can help alleviate these symptoms.

Other physical symptoms of PTSD can include headaches, dizziness, and muscle tension. These symptoms can be triggered by stress and trauma, and can significantly impact a veteran's daily life. It is important for veterans to be aware of these physical symptoms and seek support from healthcare professionals to address them. By understanding and addressing the physical symptoms of PTSD, veterans can take steps toward healing and improving their overall well-being.

For military veterans suffering from PTSD, understanding and recognizing the emotional symptoms of this condition is crucial in seeking help and managing their mental health. Emotional symptoms of PTSD can manifest in various ways, impacting the individual's daily life and relationships. It is important for veterans to be aware of these symptoms and how they can seek support to cope with them.

One common emotional symptom of PTSD in veterans is intense feelings of fear or anxiety. Veterans may experience flashbacks or nightmares related to their traumatic experiences, leading to heightened levels of stress and anxiety. These feelings can be overwhelming and interfere with their ability to function in daily life. It is important for veterans to seek professional help to address these feelings and learn healthy coping strategies.

Another emotional symptom of PTSD in veterans is anger and irritability. Veterans may feel easily agitated or angered, often lashing out at loved ones or struggling to control their emotions. This can strain relationships and lead to feelings of guilt or shame. By understanding the root of this anger and learning to communicate effectively, veterans can work towards managing their emotions and improving their relationships

Guilt and shame are also common emotional symptoms of PTSD in veterans. Many veterans may blame themselves for the traumatic events they experienced or feel ashamed of their reactions to these events. These feelings can be debilitating and prevent veterans from seeking help. It is important for veterans to recognize that these emotions are a normal part of the healing process and to seek support from mental health professionals who can help them work through these feelings

Lastly, emotional numbness is another common symptom of PTSD in veterans. Veterans may feel disconnected from their emotions, finding it difficult to experience joy or pleasure in their daily lives. This emotional numbness can impact their relationships and overall well-being. By seeking therapy and engaging in activities that bring them joy, veterans can work towards reconnecting with their emotions and finding healing from their PTSD.

Cognitive Symptoms of PTSD

Military veterans who have experienced trauma during their time of service may struggle with a range of cognitive symptoms associated with Post-Traumatic Stress Disorder (PTSD). These symptoms can impact a veteran's ability to think clearly, concentrate, and remember important details. In the sub chapter titled "Cognitive Symptoms of PTSD" in the book "Echoes of War," we will explore how these symptoms can manifest and provide strategies for managing them.

One common cognitive symptom of PTSD is difficulty concentrating. Veterans may find themselves easily distracted or unable to focus on tasks for an extended period of time. This can make it challenging to complete work assignments, engage in conversations, or even follow simple instructions. By understanding that this is a common symptom of PTSD, veterans can begin to develop coping mechanisms to improve their concentration and focus.

Another cognitive symptom of PTSD is memory problems. Veterans may struggle to remember important details, such as appointments, names, or events. This can be frustrating and lead to feelings of inadequacy or self-doubt. By utilizing memory aids, such as calendars, to-do lists, or reminders on a smartphone, veterans can improve their ability to recall important information and reduce feelings of stress and anxiety

In addition to concentration and memory issues, veterans with PTSD may also experience difficulty with decision-making. This can manifest as indecisiveness, second-guessing choices, or feeling overwhelmed by even simple decisions. By breaking down decisions into smaller, more manageable steps, veterans can reduce feelings of anxiety and make choices that align with their values and goals.

Furthermore, veterans with PTSD may struggle with negative thinking patterns, such as catastrophic or black-and-white thinking. These cognitive distortions can contribute to feelings of hopelessness, helplessness, and worthlessness. By challenging these negative thoughts and replacing them with more balanced and realistic perspectives, veterans can improve their overall mental well-being and reduce symptoms of PTSD.

In conclusion, the cognitive symptoms of PTSD can have a significant impact on military veterans' daily lives. By recognizing these symptoms and implementing strategies to manage them, veterans can improve their cognitive functioning and overall quality of life. Through self-awareness, support from mental health professionals, and a willingness to try new coping techniques, veterans can navigate the challenges of PTSD and work towards healing and recovery.

3

Facing Triggers: Loud Noises, Crowded Spaces, and Fast-Moving Vehicles

Understanding PTSD Triggers

One of the most challenging aspects of living with PTSD as a military veteran is navigating the various triggers that can exacerbate symptoms and lead to distressing episodes. These triggers can be anything from loud noises and crowded spaces to specific smells or sights that remind you of traumatic experiences. By understanding what triggers your PTSD, you can begin to take steps to manage them effectively and regain a sense of control over your symptoms.

It's important to recognize that PTSD triggers are unique to each individual and can vary greatly from person to person. For some veterans, the sound of fireworks or a car backfiring can instantly transport them back to a combat zone, triggering intense feelings of fear and anxiety. For others, certain smells or locations may trigger memories of a traumatic event, leading to a range of emotional and physical responses. By identifying your specific triggers, you can start to develop coping strategies that work best for you.

One key aspect of understanding PTSD triggers is recognizing the physical and emotional signs that indicate you are being triggered. These signs can include increased heart rate, sweating, trembling, and feelings of panic or dread. By learning to tune into your body and emotions, you can start to identify when you are being triggered and take steps to intervene before symptoms escalate. This might involve practicing deep breathing exercises, using grounding techniques, or removing yourself from the triggering situation altogether.

In addition to individual triggers, it's also important to consider the impact of cumulative stress and triggers on your overall mental health. Over time, exposure to multiple triggers can build up and contribute to a sense of overwhelm and emotional dysregulation. By being proactive in managing your triggers and seeking support when needed, you can minimize the negative effects of cumulative stress and work towards a healthier, more balanced lifestyle.

Coping Strategies for Managing Triggers

Ultimately, understanding PTSD triggers is a crucial step in the journey toward healing and recovery for military veterans living with PTSD. By identifying your triggers, recognizing the signs of being triggered, and developing effective coping strategies, you can start to regain control over your symptoms and build resilience in the face of adversity. Remember, you are not alone in this journey, and there is support available to help you navigate the challenges of living with PTSD as a veteran.

One of the most challenging aspects of living with PTSD as a military veteran is learning how to manage triggers that can set off intense emotional and physical reactions. Triggers can be anything from a loud noise that reminds you of combat to a certain smell that brings back traumatic memories. It is crucial for veterans to develop coping strategies to help them navigate these triggers and minimize their impact on daily life.

One effective coping strategy for managing triggers is to practice mindfulness and grounding techniques. By focusing on the present moment and using techniques such as deep breathing or visualization, veterans can help bring themselves back to reality when triggered. This can help prevent the escalation of emotions and physical symptoms that often accompany triggers.

Another helpful coping strategy is to establish a strong support network. Connecting with other veterans who understand what you are going through can provide a sense of camaraderie and understanding. Additionally, reaching out to mental health professionals or support groups can offer valuable resources and guidance on how to cope with triggers in a healthy way.

One of the most challenging aspects of living with post-traumatic stress disorder (PTSD) is learning how to manage triggers that can bring on intense feelings of anxiety, fear, and distress. For military veterans who have experienced trauma during their service, triggers can be especially potent and can arise unexpectedly, making it crucial to develop effective strategies for coping with them. Seeking support for trigger management is essential in helping veterans navigate the complexities of PTSD and regain a sense of control over their lives.

Engaging in regular physical activity can also be a beneficial coping strategy for managing triggers. Exercise has been shown to reduce symptoms of PTSD and can help veterans release pent-up energy and tension. Whether it's going for a run, working out, or participating in a team sport, finding a physical activity that you enjoy can be a powerful tool in managing triggers.

Finally, it is important for veterans to be patient and compassionate with themselves as they work through their triggers.

Recovery from PTSD is a journey, and setbacks are a normal part of the process. By practicing self-care, seeking support when needed, and using coping strategies consistently, veterans can learn to manage their triggers and reclaim control over their lives.

Seeking Support for Trigger Management

Many veterans may feel hesitant or embarrassed to seek help for managing triggers, but it is important to remember that seeking support is a sign of strength, not weakness. There are a variety of resources available specifically for military veterans struggling with PTSD, including therapy, support groups, and specialized treatment programs. These resources can provide veterans with the tools and guidance they need to identify their triggers, understand their reactions, and develop healthy coping mechanisms.

Therapy is often a key component in trigger management for veterans with PTSD. Cognitive behavioral therapy (CBT) and eye movement desensitization and reprocessing (EMDR) are two evidence-based therapies that have been shown to be effective in helping veterans process traumatic memories and learn to manage triggers. Working with a therapist who specializes in treating PTSD can provide veterans with a safe space to explore their triggers and develop personalized strategies for coping with them.

Support groups can also be a valuable source of support for veterans struggling with trigger management. Connecting with other veterans who have experienced similar traumas can help individuals feel less alone in their struggles and provide a sense of camaraderie and understanding. By sharing their experiences and coping strategies with others, veterans can gain new insights and perspectives on how to effectively manage their triggers.

In conclusion, seeking support for trigger management is a crucial step in the journey toward healing for military veterans with PTSD. By accessing therapy, support groups, and other resources specifically tailored to the needs of veterans, individuals can develop the skills and strategies needed to effectively manage triggers and regain control over their lives. Remember, it is never too late to seek help and support in overcoming the challenges of PTSD – you are not alone in this battle.

4

Living with Flashbacks, Nightmares, and Sleep Disturbances

Understanding Flashbacks and Their Triggers

Flashbacks are a common symptom of post-traumatic stress disorder (PTSD) that many military veterans experience. These vivid and distressing memories can be triggered by various stimuli, such as sights, sounds, smells, or even certain words. Understanding what triggers your flashbacks is crucial in managing your PTSD and finding ways to cope with them effectively.

One of the first steps in understanding flashbacks is recognizing the signs that one is about to occur. You may start to feel anxious, irritable, or disconnected from reality. Physical symptoms like sweating, shaking, or rapid heartbeat may also accompany a flashback. By being aware of these warning signs, you can take steps to prevent a full-blown flashback from occurring.

Identifying the triggers that set off your flashbacks is key to managing your PTSD. These triggers can be anything from a loud noise that reminds you of a combat situation to a certain smell that brings back memories of a traumatic event. Keeping a journal or diary of your flashbacks can help you identify patterns and common triggers, allowing you to avoid or prepare for them in the future.

Once you have identified your triggers, it is important to develop coping mechanisms to deal with flashbacks when they occur. Deep breathing exercises, mindfulness techniques, and grounding exercises can help bring you back to the present and reduce the intensity of the flashback. Seeking support from a therapist or support group can also provide you with additional tools and strategies for managing your PTSD symptoms.

Remember, you are not alone in experiencing flashbacks and PTSD. Many other military veterans have gone through similar experiences and have found ways to cope with their symptoms. By understanding your triggers, recognizing the signs of a flashback, and developing coping mechanisms, you can take control of your PTSD and begin your journey toward healing and recovery.

Coping with Nightmares and Sleep Disorders

Nightmares and sleep disorders are common symptoms of PTSD that many military veterans struggle with on a daily basis. Coping with these issues can be challenging, but with the right strategies and support, it is possible to improve the quality of your sleep and reduce the frequency of nightmares.

One of the first steps in coping with nightmares and sleep disorders is to establish a consistent bedtime routine. This can include activities such as reading a book, taking a warm bath, or practicing relaxation techniques before bed. By creating a calming environment before going to sleep, you can help signal to your body that it is time to rest and unwind.

It is also important to avoid caffeine, alcohol, and heavy meals close to bedtime, as these can disrupt your sleep and increase the likelihood of experiencing nightmares. Instead, opt for a light snack or herbal tea to help promote relaxation. Additionally, limiting screen time before bed can also improve your sleep quality, as the blue light emitted from electronic devices can interfere with your body's natural sleep-wake cycle.

If nightmares continue to disrupt your sleep despite these efforts, it may be helpful to speak with a mental health professional who specializes in treating PTSD. Cognitive behavioral therapy (CBT) has been shown to be effective in reducing the frequency and intensity of nightmares in individuals with PTSD. This type of therapy can help you identify and challenge negative thought patterns that may be contributing to your nightmares, as well as teach you relaxation techniques to use when you are experiencing distressing dreams.

Remember, you are not alone in dealing with nightmares and sleep disorders as a result of PTSD. By utilizing these coping strategies and seeking support from mental health professionals and fellow veterans, you can take steps toward improving your sleep and overall well-being. It is important to prioritize self-care and seek help when needed, as quality sleep is essential for managing symptoms of PTSD and promoting healing on your journey to recovery.

Seeking Professional Help for Sleep Disturbances

One common symptom of PTSD that many military veterans struggle with is sleep disturbances. Whether it's difficulty falling asleep, staying asleep, or experiencing nightmares, disrupted sleep can have a significant impact on a veteran's quality of life. If you find yourself struggling with sleep disturbances, it's important to seek professional help to address these issues.

One of the first steps in seeking professional help for sleep disturbances is to reach out to your primary care physician or mental health provider. They can help assess your symptoms and determine the best course of treatment for you. This may include therapy, medication, or a combination of both. It's important to be honest and open about your sleep issues so that you can receive the most effective treatment.

Therapy can be especially helpful in addressing sleep disturbances related to PTSD. Cognitive behavioral therapy (CBT) has been shown to be effective in treating insomnia and nightmares in veterans with PTSD. Through CBT, you can learn techniques to improve your sleep hygiene and manage your anxiety and stress levels, which can help improve your overall sleep quality.

In addition to therapy, medication may also be prescribed to help manage sleep disturbances. While medication can be effective in the short term, it's important to work closely with your healthcare provider to monitor any potential side effects and ensure that the medication is still necessary for your treatment plan. It's also important to explore non-pharmacological treatments, such as mindfulness and relaxation techniques, to complement your treatment.

Overall, seeking professional help for sleep disturbances related to PTSD is crucial in helping you improve your quality of life and manage your symptoms. By working closely with your healthcare provider and being proactive in addressing your sleep issues, you can take steps towards better sleep and overall well-being. Remember that you are not alone in this journey, and there are resources and support available to help you along the way

5

The Emotional Toll of PTSD: Guilt, Sorrow, and Survivor's Remorse

Exploring Survivor Guilt: A Veteran's Perspective

In this sub chapter, we will delve into the complex and often misunderstood phenomenon of survivor guilt from the perspective of a military veteran. Survivor guilt is a common experience among those who have served in the military, especially for those who have witnessed the loss of comrades in combat. It is a profound sense of guilt that can arise from surviving a dangerous or traumatic event when others did not. This guilt can be overwhelming and can lead to feelings of shame, self-blame, and even a sense of unworthiness.

For many veterans, survivor guilt is a constant companion, lurking just beneath the surface of their daily lives. It can manifest in a variety of ways, from intrusive thoughts and memories to nightmares and flashbacks. It can also lead to feelings of isolation and alienation from others, as veterans struggle to come to terms with their own survival in the face of tragedy. This sub chapter will explore the impact of survivor guilt on veterans' mental health and well-being and will offer strategies for coping with and overcoming these di cult emotions.

One of the key challenges for veterans struggling with survivor guilt is the stigma surrounding mental health in the military community. Many veterans feel pressure to project an image of strength and resilience and may be reluctant to seek help for their emotional struggles. However, it is important for veterans to recognize that survivor guilt is a normal and understandable reaction to trauma, and that seeking help is a sign of strength, not weakness. By reaching out for support from mental health professionals, fellow veterans, and support groups, veterans can begin to process their emotions and work towards healing.

It is also important for veterans to practice self-care and self-compassion as they navigate the difficult terrain of survivor guilt. This may involve engaging in activities that bring joy and relaxation, such as exercise, hobbies, or spending time with loved ones. It may also involve challenging negative thoughts and beliefs about oneself, and learning to cultivate self-compassion and forgiveness. By taking these proactive steps, veterans can begin to make peace with their past and move towards a place of acceptance and healing.

In conclusion, survivor guilt is a complex and challenging experience for many military veterans, but it is not insurmountable. By acknowledging their emotions, seeking support, and practicing self-care, veterans can begin to navigate the difficult terrain of survivor guilt and work towards healing and recovery. It is important for veterans to remember that they are not alone in their struggles and that there is help and support available to them as they journey through the aftermath of trauma.

One of the most challenging aspects of living with PTSD as a military veteran is coping with feelings of guilt and remorse. Many veterans struggle with overwhelming emotions related to their experiences in combat, leading to a cycle of self-blame and regret. It is important to recognize that these feelings are normal reactions to trauma and that there are healthy ways to cope with them.

Practicing self-care is another important aspect of coping with feelings of guilt and remorse. Engaging in activities that bring joy and relaxation, such as exercise, meditation, or spending time with loved ones, can help veterans manage their stress and improve their overall well-being. Taking care of oneself is not selfish – it is necessary for healing and recovery

First and foremost, it is crucial for veterans to seek professional help in dealing with feelings of guilt and remorse. Therapy can provide a safe space to explore these emotions and develop coping strategies to manage them effectively. Talking to a therapist who specializes in military PTSD can help veterans process their experiences and learn to forgive themselves for things that were out of their control.

In addition to therapy, veterans can also benefit from connecting with others who have shared similar experiences. Support groups for military veterans with PTSD offer a sense of camaraderie and understanding that can be incredibly healing. By sharing their stories with others who have been through similar struggles, veterans can feel less isolated and more supported in their journey towards healing.

Ultimately, it is important for veterans to remember that they are not alone in their struggles with guilt and remorse. By seeking help, connecting with others, and practicing self-care, veterans can learn to navigate these difficult emotions and move towards a place of healing and peace. It is never too late to start the journey towards self-forgiveness and acceptance.

Finding Healing and Forgiveness

As military veterans, we have all experienced trauma and hardships during our time in service. For many of us, these experiences have left deep emotional scars that can be difficult to overcome. Post-traumatic stress disorder (PTSD) is a common struggle that many veterans face, and finding healing and forgiveness can be a crucial step in our journey toward recovery.

One of the first steps towards finding healing and forgiveness is acknowledging the pain and trauma that we have experienced. It is important to recognize that it is okay to feel the way we do and that seeking help is not a sign of weakness. By confronting our past experiences and emotions, we can begin to process and heal from the wounds that have been inflicted upon us.

Forgiveness is another key aspect of finding healing from PTSD. This does not mean that we have to forget or condone the actions that have caused us harm, but rather that we release ourselves from the burden of holding onto anger and resentment. By forgiving those who have hurt us, we can free ourselves from the chains that bind us to our past traumas and begin to move forward toward a brighter future.

Seeking professional help is often necessary in the journey toward healing and forgiveness. Therapists and counselors who specialize in treating military PTSD can provide us with the tools and support we need to navigate through our emotions and experiences. Through therapy, we can learn healthy coping mechanisms and strategies to manage our symptoms and work towards a place of peace and healing.

6

Depression: A Familiar Adversary

Understanding Depression in the Context of PTSD

Depression is a common co-occurring condition with post-traumatic stress disorder (PTSD) among military veterans. It is important for veterans to understand how these two conditions interact and how they can seek help for both. Depression can exacerbate the symptoms of PTSD, making it even more challenging to cope with the daily struggles that come with the disorder. By recognizing the signs of depression and seeking appropriate treatment, veterans can improve their overall mental health and quality of life.

Many veterans with PTSD may experience symptoms of depression such as feelings of sadness, hopelessness, and worthlessness. These feelings can be overwhelming and may lead to a loss of interest in activities that were once enjoyable. Veterans may also struggle with sleep disturbances, changes in appetite, and difficulty concentrating. It is important for veterans to recognize these symptoms as potential signs of depression and to seek help from a mental health professional.

The relationship between PTSD and depression is complex

and often intertwined. PTSD can lead to feelings of isolation, guilt, and shame, which can contribute to the development of depression. On the other hand, depression can worsen the symptoms of PTSD, leading to a vicious cycle of negative thoughts and emotions. It is essential for veterans to address both conditions simultaneously in order to effectively manage their mental health.

Treatment options for veterans with co-occurring PTSD and depression may include therapy, medication, and lifestyle changes. Cognitive-behavioral therapy (CBT) has been shown to be effective in treating both conditions by helping veterans identify and challenge negative thought patterns. Medications such as antidepressants may also be prescribed to help alleviate symptoms of depression. Additionally, lifestyle changes such as regular exercise, healthy eating, and social support can play a crucial role in improving mental health.

In conclusion, understanding the relationship between PTSD and depression is essential for veterans seeking to improve their mental health. By recognizing the signs of depression and seeking appropriate treatment, veterans can break the cycle of negative thoughts and emotions that can exacerbate the symptoms of PTSD. It is important for veterans to reach out for help and to work with mental health professionals to develop a comprehensive treatment plan that addresses both conditions. With the right support and resources, veterans can learn to cope with their symptoms and live fulfilling lives after their military service.

Recognizing the Signs of Depression

As military veterans, it is important for us to be aware of the signs of depression, especially as we navigate the challenges of PTSD. Depression is a common co-occurring condition with

PTSD, and recognizing the signs early on can help us seek the appropriate help and support that we need. Some of the common signs of depression include persistent feelings of sadness, hopelessness, irritability, and loss of interest in activities that we once enjoyed. It is important to remember that depression is not a sign of weakness, but rather a medical condition that requires treatment.

One of the key signs of depression in military veterans is the feeling of isolation and withdrawal from family and friends. Many of us may feel disconnected from our loved ones and struggle to open up about our emotions and experiences. This can further exacerbate feelings of loneliness and despair, making it crucial to reach out for help and support. Additionally, changes in sleep patterns, appetite, and energy levels can also be indicators of depression. If you find yourself struggling with these symptoms, it is important to seek help from a mental health professional who can provide you with the necessary resources and support.

Another important sign of depression in military veterans is the presence of physical symptoms such as headaches, stomach issues, and muscle pains. These physical symptoms are often linked to the emotional distress that comes with depression and PTSD. It is crucial to address both the physical and emotional aspects of depression in order to achieve holistic healing and recovery. Additionally, thoughts of self-harm or suicide should never be taken lightly and should be addressed immediately by seeking help from a mental health professional or contacting a crisis hotline.

It is important for military veterans to recognize that seeking help for depression is not a sign of weakness, but rather a courageous step towards healing and recovery. By acknowledging the signs of depression and reaching out for support, we can begin to break free from the cycle of despair and isolation that often accompanies this condition. Remember that you are not alone in your struggles, and there are resources and professionals available to help you navigate through this difficult time. Take the first step towards healing by recognizing the signs of depression and seeking the help that you deserve.

In conclusion, recognizing the signs of depression is crucial for military veterans as we navigate through the challenges of PTSD. By being aware of the common symptoms of depression and reaching out for support, we can begin to heal and recover from the emotional and physical toll that this condition can take on us. Remember that seeking help is a sign of strength, not weakness, and that there are professionals and resources available to support you on your journey toward recovery. You are not alone in your struggles, and there is hope for a brighter future ahead.

Seeking Treatment and Support for Depression

As a military veteran struggling with PTSD, it is important to remember that seeking treatment and support for depression is not a sign of weakness, but rather a courageous step towards healing and recovery. Depression is a common concurring condition with PTSD, and it is crucial to address it in order to effectively manage your symptoms and improve your overall well-being.

One of the first steps in seeking treatment for depression is to reach out to a mental health professional who is experienced in working with veterans and understands the unique challenges they face. This may include a psychologist, psychiatrist, or counselor who can provide therapy, medication management, or a combination of both. It is important to nd a provider whom you feel comfortable with and whom you trust to guide you through the treatment process.

In addition to individual therapy, group therapy can also be a valuable resource for veterans struggling with depression. Connecting with other veterans who have similar experiences can provide a sense of camaraderie and support, and can help combat feelings of isolation and loneliness. Group therapy can also provide opportunities to learn new coping skills and strategies for managing depression symptoms.

In addition to professional treatment, it is important to build a strong support network of friends, family, and fellow veterans who can offer emotional support and encouragement. Talking openly and honestly about your struggles with depression can help to reduce feelings of shame and stigma, and can help you feel less alone in your journey towards healing. Building connections with others who understand what you are going through can provide a sense of belonging and validation

Remember, seeking treatment and support for depression is a brave and important step in your journey toward healing from PTSD. By reaching out for help, you are taking control of your mental health and well-being, and setting yourself on a path towards a brighter and more fulfilling future. You are not alone in this battle, and there are resources and support available to help you through this challenging time.

7

The Strain on Relationships: Navigating Marriage and Family Dynamics

Communicating with Loved Ones about PTSD

One of the most challenging aspects of living with PTSD as a military veteran is communicating with loved ones about your experiences and struggles. It can be difficult to open up about the trauma you have endured and the impact it has had on your mental health. However, building a strong support system that includes your family and friends is crucial for your overall well-being and recovery.

When discussing your PTSD with loved ones, it is important to be honest and open about your feelings and experiences. It can be helpful to educate them about the symptoms of PTSD and how it affects their daily life. By providing them with a better understanding of your condition, they will be better equipped to offer you the support and understanding you need.

Overall, building open and honest communication with your loved ones about your PTSD is essential for your mental health and well-being. By sharing your experiences and feelings with those closest to you, you can strengthen your support system and work towards healing and recovery together. Remember, you are not alone in this journey, and your loved ones are there to support you every step of the way.

Managing Relationship Challenges Caused by PTSD

It is also important to set boundaries when communicating with loved ones about your PTSD. Let them know what triggers your symptoms and what support you need during di cult times. This can help prevent misunderstandings and conflicts that may arise from a lack of communication.

Additionally, it is important to practice active listening when talking to loved ones about your PTSD. Allow them to express their thoughts and feelings about your condition without judgment. Remember that everyone processes trauma differently, and it is important to be patient and understanding with your loved ones as they navigate this new aspect of your life.

Military veterans face unique challenges when it comes to managing relationships, especially when dealing with the effects of post-traumatic stress disorder (PTSD). The symptoms of PTSD, such as hyperarousal, avoidance, and flashbacks, can make it difficult to maintain healthy relationships with loved ones. However, there are strategies that veterans can employ to help navigate these challenges and strengthen their connections with others.

One key aspect of managing relationship challenges caused by PTSD is communication. It's important for veterans to communicate openly and honestly with their loved ones about their struggles and how PTSD impacts their behavior. By sharing their experiences and feelings, veterans can help their partners and family members better understand what they are going through and offer support in a meaningful way.

Another important strategy is setting boundaries. Veterans

with PTSD may have triggers that can cause distress or anxiety, and it's crucial for them to communicate these triggers to their loved ones. By setting boundaries and establishing clear expectations, veterans can create a safe and supportive environment for themselves and their relationships.

Additionally, seeking professional help is essential for managing relationship challenges caused by PTSD. Therapists and counselors can provide veterans with the tools and coping mechanisms they need to navigate their symptoms and improve their communication skills. Couples therapy or family therapy can also be beneficial for addressing relationship issues and strengthening bonds.

Overall, managing relationship challenges caused by PTSD requires patience, understanding, and a willingness to work together with loved ones. By prioritizing communication, setting boundaries, and seeking professional help, veterans can overcome the obstacles that PTSD presents in their relationships and build stronger, more resilient connections with those they care about. Remember, you are not alone in this journey, and there is help available to support you every step of the way.

Strengthening Family Bonds Through Support and Understanding

As military veterans, we understand the unique challenges that come with serving our country. One of the most common struggles that many of us face is post-traumatic stress disorder (PTSD). This condition can have a profound impact on our lives, as well as the lives of our loved ones. In order to overcome this challenge, it is crucial to strengthen family bonds through support and understanding.

Support from family members can make a world of difference for veterans struggling with PTSD. By providing a listening ear, a shoulder to lean on, and a helping hand when needed, family members can create a safe and nurturing environment for their loved ones. This support can help veterans feel less isolated and more connected to their loved ones, which can be incredibly healing.

Understanding is also key when it comes to supporting a veteran with PTSD. Family members should take the time to educate themselves about the condition and its symptoms, so they can better understand what their loved one is going through. By showing empathy and compassion, family members can help veterans feel validated and supported in their journey toward healing.

Communication is another essential component of strengthening family bonds when dealing with PTSD. By creating an open and honest dialogue, family members can work together to address any challenges that may arise. This can help prevent misunderstandings and conflicts, and instead foster a sense of unity and cooperation within the family.

Ultimately, by strengthening family bonds through support and understanding, veterans with PTSD can feel more empowered and encouraged to seek help and work toward recovery. By coming together as a family unit, we can create a strong support system that enables veterans to overcome their struggles and thrive in their post-military lives. Through love, empathy, and communication, we can build a foundation of healing and resilience that will benefit not only the veteran but the entire family as well.

8

Seeking Help: Resources and Support for Veterans with PTSD

Understanding Treatment Options for PTSD

Military veterans who have experienced trauma during their service may find themselves struggling with post-traumatic stress disorder (PTSD). It is important for veterans to understand that there are various treatment options available to help them cope with their symptoms and improve their quality of life. In this sub chapter, we will explore some of the most commonly used treatment options for PTSD in military veterans.

One of the most effective treatment options for PTSD is therapy, specifically cognitive-behavioral therapy (CBT). CBT helps veterans identify and challenge negative thought patterns and behaviors that contribute to their PTSD symptoms. By working with a trained therapist, veterans can learn new coping mechanisms and strategies to manage their symptoms and improve their overall mental health.

Another common treatment option for PTSD is medication. While medication alone is not usually enough to treat PTSD effectively, it can be a helpful tool when used in conjunction with therapy. Antidepressants and anti-anxiety medications are often prescribed to help manage symptoms such as depression, anxiety, and insomnia. It is important for veterans to work closely with their healthcare provider to find the right medication and dosage that works best for them. Medication is not always the best option. It needs to be taken seriously and used properly and often used as a last resort.

In addition to therapy and medication, other treatment options for PTSD in military veterans include eye movement desensitization and reprocessing (EMDR) therapy, group therapy, and alternative therapies such as mindfulness, and acupuncture. EMDR therapy involves a series of guided eye movements that help veterans process traumatic memories and reduce the emotional distress associated with them. Group therapy allows veterans to connect with others who have similar experiences and provide support and encouragement to one another.

Overall, it is crucial for military veterans struggling with PTSD to seek help and explore the various treatment options available to them. Each person is different, and what works for one veteran may not necessarily work for another. By working closely with healthcare providers and mental health professionals, veterans can find the right combination of treatments that will help them heal and move forward in their journey toward recovery. Remember, there is hope and help available for those who are willing to reach out and take the necessary steps toward healing from PTSD.

Navigating the VA System: Accessing Support Services

As military veterans, we have sacrificed so much for our country, and it is only right that we have access to the support services we need as we transition back to civilian life. The VA system can be overwhelming to navigate, but it is important to take advantage of the resources available to us. From mental health services to disability benefits, the VA offers a variety of programs to help us cope with the challenges of post-traumatic stress disorder (PTSD).

One of the first steps in accessing support services through the VA is to reach out to your local VA medical center or clinic. They can provide you with information on the services available to you and help you navigate the system. It is important to be proactive in seeking help for your PTSD, as early intervention can lead to better outcomes in the long run. Don't hesitate to ask for assistance – the VA is there to support you.

Once you have connected with your local VA center, you may be eligible for a range of mental health services, including individual therapy, group therapy, and medication management. These services can help you manage the symptoms of PTSD and improve your quality of life. Additionally, the VA offers specialized programs for veterans with PTSD, such as cognitive processing therapy and prolonged exposure therapy. These evidence-based treatments are effective in reducing PTSD symptoms and improving overall mental health.

In addition to mental health services, the VA also provides disability benefits for veterans with service-connected disabilities, including PTSD. These benefits can help offset the financial burden of living with a disability and ensure that you have access to the care and support you need. To apply for disability benefits, you will need to submit a claim to the VA, providing evidence of your service-connected disability and how it impacts your daily life. The process can be complex, but there are resources available to help you navigate it.

Overall, accessing support services through the VA can be a crucial step in your journey towards healing from PTSD. By taking advantage of the resources available to you, you can improve your mental health, quality of life, and overall well-being. Remember, you are not alone in this journey – the VA is here to support you every step of the way. Don't hesitate to reach out for help and take control of your mental health.

Seeking Community and Peer Support

Military veterans who have experienced the trauma of war often find themselves struggling with the invisible wounds of post traumatic stress disorder (PTSD). The journey to healing from these wounds can be a long and difficult one, but seeking out community and peer support can make a world of difference. Connecting with others who have shared similar experiences can provide a sense of understanding and camaraderie that is essential for healing.

One of the most powerful ways for military veterans to seek community and peer support is through support groups specifically tailored to those who have served in the military. These groups provide a safe space for veterans to share their stories, struggles, and successes with others who can truly relate. Being able to connect with peers who have walked in their shoes can provide a sense of validation and belonging that is crucial for healing from the effects of PTSD.

In addition to support groups, many veterans find solace in connecting with other veterans through online forums and social media groups. These virtual communities offer a way for veterans to reach out for support and advice, even if they are unable to attend in-person meetings. The ability to connect with others who understand the unique challenges of military service can provide a sense of solidarity and comfort that is invaluable in the healing process.

Peer support can also come in the form of one-on-one relationships with other veterans who have been through similar experiences. These connections can provide a sense of mentorship and guidance, as well as a listening ear for veterans who may be struggling with the effects of PTSD. Building these relationships can help veterans feel less isolated and more supported as they navigate their journey toward healing.

In conclusion, seeking community and peer support is an essential part of the healing process for military veterans who are living with PTSD. By connecting with others who understand their experiences, veterans can find a sense of belonging and validation that is crucial for their mental health and well-being. Whether through support groups, online communities, or one-on-one relationships, reaching out for support can make a world of difference in the journey toward healing from the scars of war.

9

The Isolation and Withdrawal of PTSD

Understanding the Impact of Isolation on Mental Health

Isolation is a common experience for many military veterans who have returned from deployment. Whether it be physical isolation from friends and family or emotional isolation due to the invisible scars of war, the impact on mental health can be profound. In this sub chapter, we will explore the ways in which isolation can exacerbate symptoms of PTSD and other mental health conditions, and offer strategies for combating the negative effects of isolation.

One of the key ways in which isolation can impact mental health is through a sense of disconnection from others. Many veterans who have experienced trauma during their service may find it difficult to relate to civilians or even other veterans who have not had similar experiences. This can lead to feelings of loneliness and alienation, which can worsen symptoms of PTSD and depression. By understanding the impact of isolation on mental health, veterans can begin to take steps to reconnect with others and build a support network that can help them cope with their experiences.

Isolation can also lead to feelings of shame and guilt, which are common symptoms of PTSD. Veterans may feel like they are burdening others with their struggles, or that they are somehow weak for not being able to cope on their own. This can further exacerbate feelings of isolation and make it harder for veterans to seek help. By recognizing and challenging these negative beliefs, veterans can begin to break free from the cycle of isolation and shame that can keep them trapped in their struggles.

In addition to the emotional impact of isolation, there are also physical consequences that can affect mental health. Chronic isolation has been linked to an increased risk of developing anxiety, depression, and even cognitive decline. By understanding the impact of isolation on mental health, veterans can take proactive steps to stay connected with others and engage in activities that promote mental well-being. This may include joining a support group, participating in therapy, or simply reaching out to a friend or loved one for support.

Overall, it is important for military veterans to recognize the impact that isolation can have on their mental health and take steps to combat its negative effects. By building a strong support network, challenging negative beliefs, and engaging in activities that promote mental well-being, veterans can begin to break free from the cycle of isolation and nd healing and connection in their lives. It is never too late to reach out for help and start the journey towards recovery and resilience.

Coping Strategies for Combating Isolation

One of the most common challenges that military veterans face when dealing with PTSD is the feeling of isolation. This can be exacerbated by the fact that many veterans may have difficulty relating to civilians who have not experienced the same traumas and struggles. However, it is important for veterans to remember that they are not alone in their experiences and that there are coping strategies that can help combat feelings of isolation.

One effective coping strategy for combating isolation is to seek out support from other veterans who have also experienced PTSD. This can be done through support groups, online forums, or veterans-specific therapy programs. Connecting with others who have been through similar experiences can help veterans feel understood and less alone in their struggles.

Another helpful coping strategy is to engage in activities that promote social connection and interaction. This can include joining a sports team, volunteering in the community, or participating in group therapy sessions. By engaging in activities that involve others, veterans can combat feelings of isolation and build a supportive network of peers.

It is also important for veterans to prioritize self-care and mental health. This can include practicing mindfulness and relaxation techniques, engaging in regular exercise, and seeking professional help when needed. Taking care of one's mental and emotional well-being can help combat feelings of isolation and promote overall wellness.

Lastly, veterans should remember that it is okay to ask for help when needed. Seeking support from friends, family, or mental health professionals is not a sign of weakness, but a proactive step towards healing and recovery. By reaching out for help and utilizing coping strategies, veterans can combat feelings of isolation and work towards building a fulfilling and connected life after military service.

Building a Supportive Network

As military veterans, we often face unique challenges that

can be difficult to navigate on our own. One of the most important things we can do for ourselves is to build a supportive network of individuals who understand what we are going through. This network can include fellow veterans, mental health professionals, family members, and friends who are willing to listen and offer support when we need it most.

When it comes to dealing with military PTSD, having a supportive network is crucial. By surrounding ourselves with people who understand our experiences, we can feel less alone and more understood. This can help us feel more comfortable opening up about our struggles and seeking help when we need it. Whether it's attending support groups, connecting with other veterans online, or reaching out to a therapist, having a strong network can make a world of difference in our journey toward healing.

Building a supportive network is not always easy, especially for those of us who may struggle with trust issues or have difficulty asking for help. It's important to remember that there are people out there who genuinely care about our well-being and want to help us through our challenges. By taking small steps to reach out and connect with others, we can slowly build a network of support that can help us through the tough times.

In addition to seeking support from others, it's also important for us to be willing to offer support to our fellow veterans who may be struggling with military PTSD. By being there for others, we can create a sense of community and solidarity that can help us all feel more understood and less alone in our struggles. Whether it's offering a listening ear, sharing resources, or simply being there for someone in their time of need, we can all play a role in building a more supportive network for military veterans.

In the end, building a supportive network is an essential part of our journey through PTSD. By connecting with others who understand our experiences, we can feel less isolated and more empowered to seek help and work toward healing. Remember, you are not alone in this journey, and there are people out there who are ready and willing to support you every step of the way.

10

Survivor Guilt: The Burden We Carry

Exploring the Complexities of Survivor Guilt

Survivor guilt is a common and complex emotion that many military veterans experience after returning from combat. It is a feeling of guilt or remorse for surviving a traumatic event when others did not. This emotion can be overwhelming and difficult to process, leading to symptoms of post traumatic stress disorder (PTSD). In this sub chapter, we will explore the complexities of survivor guilt and how it can impact veterans who have served in the military.

One of the key aspects of survivor guilt is the belief that one does not deserve to live when others have died. This can lead to feelings of shame, self-blame, and worthlessness. Veterans may struggle with the question of "Why me?" and feel a sense of responsibility for the lives lost in combat. These feelings can be debilitating and can worsen symptoms of PTSD, such as flashbacks, nightmares, and hyper vigilance.

In conclusion, survivor guilt is a complex emotion that many military veterans experience after returning from combat. It can have a profound impact on their mental health and well-being, exacerbating symptoms of PTSD and hindering their ability to heal. By exploring the complexities of survivor guilt and seeking support from therapists and fellow veterans, individuals can begin to process these feelings and learn to cope with them in a healthy way.

Survivor guilt can also manifest in the form of avoidance behaviors. Veterans may try to numb their feelings of guilt by avoiding reminders of the traumatic event or isolating them-selves from others. This can create a cycle of isolation and self-destructive behavior, further exacerbating their PTSD symptoms. It is important for veterans to seek support and therapy to address these feelings of guilt and learn healthy coping mechanisms.

Another aspect of survivor guilt is the impact it can have on relationships. Veterans may struggle to connect with loved ones and feel disconnected from those around them. They may fear judgment or rejection from others who do not understand their experiences. This can lead to feelings of loneliness and isolation, making it even more difficult to process their emotions and heal from their trauma.

It is important for veterans to remember that they are not alone in their struggles and that there is help available to support them on their journey to healing.

Coping Strategies for Managing Survivor Guilt

Survivor guilt is a common and complex emotion that many military veterans experience after returning from combat. It is the feeling of guilt or shame that arises from having survived a traumatic event when others did not. This can be especially challenging for veterans who have lost comrades in battle, as they may struggle with feelings of unworthiness or a sense of responsibility for their fallen comrades. Coping with survivor guilt is an important part of the healing process for veterans dealing with PTSD.

One coping strategy for managing survivor guilt is to seek support from fellow veterans who have also experienced similar feelings. Connecting with others who understand the unique challenges of military service can provide a sense of camaraderie and validation. Support groups, therapy, or online forums can be valuable resources for veterans looking to share their experiences and receive support from others who can relate to their struggles.

Another helpful coping strategy is to practice self-care and prioritize mental health. This can include engaging in activities that bring joy and relaxation, such as exercise, meditation, or spending time with loved ones. Taking care of oneself physically and emotionally can help veterans build resilience and cope with the difficult emotions that come with survivor guilt.

It can also be beneficial for veterans to challenge negative thoughts and beliefs that contribute to feelings of guilt or shame. Cognitive-behavioral therapy techniques, such as re-framing negative thoughts or practicing self-compassion, can help veterans change their perspective and develop more adaptive ways of thinking about their experiences. By challenging distorted thinking patterns, veterans can begin to release themselves from the grip of survivor guilt.

Finally, seeking professional help from a therapist or counselor who specializes in treating PTSD and survivor guilt can be an important step in managing these difficult emotions. Therapy can provide veterans with tools and techniques for coping with survivor guilt, as well as a safe space to process their feelings and experiences. A mental health professional can offer guidance and support as veterans work through their emotions and begin to heal from their trauma. By taking proactive steps to address survivor guilt, veterans can work towards finding peace and acceptance in their post-military lives.

Finding Meaning and Purpose in Survival

For military veterans who have experienced the horrors of war, finding meaning and purpose in survival can be a challenging and ongoing journey. Many veterans struggle with PTSD, a condition that can make it difficult to find a sense of purpose or direction in life after returning home from combat. However, it is possible to find meaning and purpose in survival, even in the face of the most difficult circumstances.

One way to find meaning and purpose in survival is to connect with other veterans who have experienced similar challenges. By sharing your experiences with others who understand what you have been through, you can gain a sense of validation and camaraderie that can help you feel less alone in your struggles. Support groups, therapy sessions, and online forums can all be valuable resources for connecting with other veterans and finding a sense of purpose in your survival.

Another way to find meaning and purpose in survival is to focus on helping others who are struggling with similar challenges. By reaching out to fellow veterans who are dealing with PTSD or other issues related to their military service, you can provide support, guidance, and understanding that can make a real difference in their lives. By using your own experiences to help others, you can find a sense of purpose and fulfillment that can help you heal and move forward.

Finding meaning and purpose in survival can also involve setting goals and working towards achieving them. Whether it's pursuing a new career, starting a family, or engaging in a hobby or passion, setting goals can give you a sense of direction and motivation that can help you move past the challenges of PTSD and find fulfillment in your life. By setting realistic and achievable goals, you can create a sense of purpose and meaning that can help you overcome the obstacles in your path.

Ultimately, finding meaning and purpose in survival is a deeply personal journey that will look different for each individual. By connecting with other veterans, helping those in need, setting goals, and seeking professional help when needed, military veterans can find a sense of purpose and fulfillment in their survival that can help them heal and move forward in their lives. Remember, you are not alone in your struggles, and there is hope and support available to help you find meaning and purpose in your survival.

11

Moving Forward: Healing and Recovery

Embracing the Journey of Healing

In this subchapter, "Embracing the Journey of Healing," we will explore the importance of acknowledging and accepting the challenges that come with PTSD as a military veteran. It is crucial to understand that healing is a process that takes time and patience. As veterans, we have been through experiences that most people cannot imagine, and it is important to give ourselves grace as we navigate through the healing journey.

One of the first steps in embracing the journey of healing is to seek support from fellow veterans who understand what you are going through. Connecting with others who have similar experiences can provide a sense of camaraderie and understanding that is crucial for healing. Whether it be through support groups, therapy, or simply talking to a trusted friend, finding a community of support can make a world of difference in the healing process.

It is also important to remember that healing is not a linear process. There will be good days and bad days, setbacks and breakthroughs. It is important to be patient with yourself and allow yourself to feel all of the emotions that come with healing. It is okay to have moments of anger, sadness, and frustration. Embracing these emotions and allowing yourself to feel them fully is a crucial step in the healing journey.

As military veterans, we have been conditioned to be strong and resilient, but it is important to remember that vulnerability is also a strength. Being vulnerable and open about your struggles with PTSD can help you connect with others and receive the support you need to heal. Embracing vulnerability is a powerful tool in the healing process and can help you build resilience and strength in the face of adversity.

In conclusion, embracing the journey of healing as a military veteran with PTSD is a courageous and important step towards reclaiming your life and finding peace. By seeking support, being patient with yourself, allowing yourself to feel all of your emotions, and embracing vulnerability, you can navigate through the healing process with grace and resilience. Remember that you are not alone in this journey, and there is a community of fellow veterans who are here to support you every step of the way.

Setting Goals for Recovery and Growth

Setting goals for recovery and growth is a crucial step in the journey toward healing from the invisible wounds of war. For military veterans struggling with PTSD, it can be challenging to envision a future beyond the pain and trauma that haunts them. However, setting goals can provide a sense of purpose and direction, helping to navigate the path toward recovery.

When setting goals for recovery and growth, it is important to start small and build upon successes. Begin by identifying specific areas of your life that have been impacted by PTSD, whether it be relationships, work, or mental health. Focus on setting realistic and achievable goals that are tailored to your individual needs and circumstances. This could range from attending therapy regularly to improving communication with loved ones or pursuing a new hobby or interest.

It is also essential to seek support from mental health professionals, fellow veterans, and loved ones when setting goals for recovery and growth. Surrounding yourself with a strong support system can provide encouragement, accountability, and guidance as you work towards your goals. Additionally, sharing your goals with others can help to keep you motivated and on track, while also fostering a sense of connection and community.

As you progress on your journey towards recovery and growth, it is important to celebrate small victories along the way. Recognize and acknowledge the progress you have made, no matter how small it may seem. This can help to boost your confidence and motivation, reinforcing your commitment to your goals. Remember, healing from PTSD is a journey, and setbacks are a natural part of the process. Be kind to yourself and practice self-compassion as you navigate the ups and downs of recovery.

In conclusion, setting goals for recovery and growth is a powerful tool for military veterans grappling with PTSD. By identifying specific areas of your life that need attention, setting realistic and achievable goals, seeking support from others, and celebrating small victories, you can create a road map toward healing and transformation. Remember, you are not alone in this journey, and with dedication, perseverance, and support, you can overcome the challenges of PTSD and thrive in your life beyond the battlefield.

Cultivating Resilience and Finding Hope

Cultivating Resilience and Finding Hope is a crucial aspect of healing for military veterans struggling with PTSD. It is essential for veterans to understand that resilience is not about bouncing back from trauma, but rather about developing the strength to face challenges head-on and adapt to life after experiencing trauma. By cultivating resilience, veterans can learn to cope with their symptoms and nd hope for a brighter future.

One way to cultivate resilience is by seeking support from fellow veterans who understand the unique challenges of military PTSD. Connecting with others who have similar experiences can provide a sense of camaraderie and understanding that is crucial for healing. Support groups, therapy sessions, and online forums can all be valuable resources for veterans looking to build resilience and find hope in their journey toward recovery.

In addition to seeking support from others, veterans can also cultivate resilience by practicing self-care and developing healthy coping mechanisms. This may include engaging in activities that bring joy and relaxation, such as exercise, meditation, or spending time in nature. By taking care of their physical and emotional well-being, veterans can build the strength and resilience needed to navigate the challenges of living with PTSD.

Finding hope is another important aspect of healing for military veterans with PTSD. It is easy to feel overwhelmed and hopeless when struggling with the symptoms of PTSD, but it is essential to remember that recovery is possible. By setting small, achievable goals and focusing on the positive aspects of life, veterans can begin to see a glimmer of hope for their future.

Overall, cultivating resilience and finding hope are essential components of healing for military veterans struggling with PTSD. By seeking support from others, practicing self-care, and focusing on the positive aspects of life, veterans can begin to build the strength and resilience needed to overcome the challenges of living with PTSD. With dedication and perseverance, veterans can find hope for a brighter future and begin their journey toward healing and recovery.

12

Conclusion

Finding Strength in Faith: For many veterans, faith has been a source of solace and strength in the darkest of times. Turning to God and seeking comfort in prayer can provide a sense of peace and guidance on the journey toward healing.

For many veterans, faith has played a crucial role in their journey towards healing from the invisible wounds of war. The struggles they face upon returning home can often feel insurmountable, but turning to their faith can provide a sense of solace and strength in the darkest of times. In moments of despair, many veterans have found comfort in prayer and a connection to God, which has helped guide them through the challenges of living with PTSD.

The journey toward healing from PTSD is a long and arduous one, but having faith can provide a sense of hope and purpose along the way. By turning to God and seeking guidance through prayer, veterans can find a sense of peace amidst the turmoil of their minds. The power of faith lies in its ability to provide comfort and reassurance, even in the face of overwhelming darkness.

For many veterans, their faith has been a source of strength that has helped them navigate the complexities of living with PTSD. By finding solace in their beliefs and seeking guidance from a higher God, they have been able to find the courage to confront their trauma and begin the healing process. Faith can provide a sense of grounding and stability amid chaos, allowing veterans to find the strength they need to move forward.

A Community of Believers: Connecting with fellow believers and engaging in prayer communities can offer invaluable support and encouragement during the recovery process. Building a network of support rooted in faith can help veterans feel less alone in their struggles

In times of despair, it can be easy to lose sight of the light at the end of the tunnel. However, for many veterans, their faith has been a beacon of hope that has guided them through even the darkest of times. By turning to God and finding comfort in prayer, they have been able to find the strength to face their demons head-on and begin the journey toward healing.

In the battle against PTSD, faith can be a powerful weapon that provides veterans with the strength and resilience they need to overcome their struggles. By finding solace in their beliefs and seeking guidance from God, veterans can find the courage to confront their trauma and take the first steps toward healing. Faith can be a source of comfort and guidance in the face of adversity, helping veterans to navigate the challenges of living with PTSD and ultimately find peace within themselves.

As military veterans navigate the challenging journey of healing from PTSD, it is crucial for them to connect with a community of believers who can offer invaluable support and encouragement. Engaging in prayer communities and building relationships with fellow believers can provide a sense of camaraderie and understanding that is essential for the recovery process. By surrounding themselves with individuals who share their faith and values, veterans can feel less isolated in their struggles and find comfort in knowing that they are not alone.

Being part of a community of believers can also offer practical support for veterans as they work through their PTSD. Whether it is through attending church services together, participating in group prayer sessions, or simply sharing their experiences, connecting with fellow believers can help veterans feel heard and understood. This sense of belonging can be a powerful source of strength and motivation as they navigate the ups and downs of the recovery process.

In addition to emotional and spiritual support, engaging with a community of believers can also provide veterans with opportunities for personal growth and healing. By participating in group discussions, Bible studies, or other faith-based activities, veterans can gain new perspectives on their experiences and learn coping strategies that are rooted in their faith. This holistic approach to healing can help veterans address the underlying issues that contribute to their PTSD and empower them to move forward with hope and resilience.

Furthermore, building a network of support rooted in faith can help veterans cultivate a sense of purpose and meaning in their recovery journey. By connecting with fellow believers who share their commitment to serving God, veterans can find inspiration and encouragement to overcome their struggles and live with intention. This shared sense of purpose can be a powerful motivator for veterans as they work towards healing and finding peace in their lives.

In conclusion, connecting with a community of believers

can offer military veterans a sense of belonging, practical support, personal growth, and a renewed sense of purpose as they navigate the challenges of PTSD recovery. By engaging with fellow believers and participating in faith-based activities, veterans can nd comfort, strength, and hope in their journey toward healing. In the words of Psalm 147:3, "He heals the brokenhearted and binds up their wounds." May veterans find solace and healing in the embrace of their faith community as they work towards overcoming their battle scars.

Trusting in God's Plan: Ultimately, placing trust in God's plan and surrendering to His will can offer a sense of reassurance and hope for the future. By relinquishing control and placing their burdens in God's hands, veterans can find the strength to persevere and overcome even the greatest challenges.

It can be incredibly difficult for veterans to let go of the need to control every aspect of their lives, especially when they have experienced such intense trauma. However, by relinquishing that control and placing their burdens in God's hands, they can experience a newfound sense of freedom and release. Trusting in God's plan means acknowledging that there is a higher power at work, guiding and protecting them through the storms of life. It is a powerful act of faith that can offer solace and comfort in times of distress.

In the tumultuous journey of recovering from PTSD, military veterans often find themselves grappling with feelings of uncertainty and fear about the future. The scars of war can run deep, leaving lasting emotional wounds that can be hard to heal. However, in the midst of the darkness, there is a beacon of hope that shines through - trusting in God's plan. By surrendering to His will and placing their trust in Him, veterans can find a sense of reassurance and peace that surpasses all understanding.

Placing trust in God's plan does not mean that veterans will be exempt from experiencing pain or hardship. In fact, it is often through the trials and challenges that they can grow stronger in their faith and resilience. By leaning on God for strength and guidance, veterans can nd the courage to face their fears head-on and push through the obstacles that stand in their way. It is a journey of faith that requires patience, perseverance, and unwavering trust in God's goodness.

Trusting in God's plan can also provide veterans with a sense of purpose and direction in their lives. It can help them see beyond their pain and suffering, to a greater purpose that is unfolding before them. By surrendering to His will, veterans can find clarity and peace in knowing that they are not alone in their struggles. God's plan for their lives is one of redemption and restoration, where beauty can emerge from the ashes of their past traumas.

Ultimately, placing trust in God's plan can offer military veterans a sense of hope for the future. It is a powerful reminder that they are not defined by their wounds, but by the strength and resilience that lies within them. By surrendering to His will and allowing Him to work in their lives, veterans can find the courage to face each day with renewed faith and determination. Trusting in God's plan is a journey of healing and transformation, where veterans can find peace and solace in the midst of their struggles with PTSD.

Epilogue

As we reach the conclusion of "Echoes of War: Healing the Wounds of PTSD," I am reminded of the power of storytelling to illuminate the darkest corners of the human experience. Throughout these pages, we have traversed the landscape of trauma and resilience, confronting the echoes of war with courage and compassion.

But our journey does not end here. For every veteran grappling with the invisible scars of combat, for every individual touched by the ripple effects of trauma, the path to healing continues. It is my hope that this book serves as a guiding light—a reminder that you are not alone, and that healing is possible.

As you close these pages and embark on your own journey, may you carry with you the lessons learned, the stories shared, and the hope kindled within these words. May you find strength in the knowledge that you are part of a community bound by shared experiences and united in the pursuit of healing.

Thank you for joining me on this profound journey. May you walk your path with courage, compassion, and resilience, knowing that the echoes of war can be silenced, and that a brighter tomorrow awaits.

Afterword

As I reflect on the completion of "Echoes of War: Healing the Wounds of PTSD," I am filled with a profound sense of gratitude and humility. This book has been a labor of love—a testament to the resilience of the human spirit and the power of community in overcoming adversity.

To all those who have shared their stories, offered their support, and walked this journey with me, I extend my deepest thanks. Your courage, vulnerability, and unwavering commitment to healing have inspired me beyond measure.

As we part ways, I urge you to carry the message of hope and healing forward into your own lives and communities. Let us continue to support and uplift one another, to confront the echoes of war with compassion and understanding, and to strive for a future where all veterans can find the peace and healing they deserve.

Thank you for allowing me to share a piece of my heart with you. May the echoes of our collective journey resonate far and wide, serving as a beacon of hope for all those who seek healing and renewal.

www.ingramcontent.com/pod-product-compliance
Lightning Source LLC
Chambersburg PA
CBHW070317160726
47999CB00003B/1065